PAIN EXPLAINED

PAIN EXPLAINED

Richard Gamlin MPhil RN DipNurs(London) CertEd FETC

Senior Lecturer Practitioner, St Benedict's Hospice, Monkwearmouth Hospital, Sunderland and the University of Sunderland

Tim Lovel BM BCh FRCP Hon DSc

Professor of Palliative Care, St Benedict's Hospice, Monkwearmouth Hospital, Sunderland

ALTMAN

Published by Altman Publishing, 65 Lake View, Egware, Middlesex, HA8 7SA, UK

First edition 2002

Typeset in 10/12 Optima by Scribe Design, Gillingham, Kent
Printed in Great Britain by George Over Ltd, Rugby

ISBN 1 86036 019X

A catalogue record for this book is available from the British Library

∞ Printed on acid-free text paper, manufactured in accordance with ANSI/NISO Z39.48-1992 (Permanence of Paper)

For Mari

CONTENTS

ABOUT THE AUTHORS

Richard Gamlin MPhil, RN, Dip Nurs (London), CertEd, FETC qualified as a nurse in 1977, and has worked in the area of palliative care in various hospitals in north-east England. Since 1985, he has worked as a lecturer in the hospice movement, and is currently responsible for planning and delivering palliative care courses to professionals and volunteers. He has worked in Eastern Europe, and has helped in the development of palliative care services.

Tim Lovel BM, BCh, FRCP, Hon DSc qualified in Medicine at Oxford in 1961. After working at the Radcliffe Infirmary and the Hammersmith Hospital he went into general practice in Hampshire for 24 years. The influence and teaching of Dame Cicely Saunders OM caused him to develop an increasing interest in the Hospice movement, and eventually to change careers. He became the consultant physician at St. Benedict's Hospice in 1988, and later also at hospices in Stockton, Hartlepool and Jarrow. A personal Chair in palliative care was awarded to him by the University of Sunderland in 1995, and an honorary DSc in 2001. He retired from clinical work in 2000, but continues with teaching activities in Britain and Eastern Europe.

1   INTRODUCTION

Everyone experiences some pain throughout their lives for many different reasons. If you think back over the past 6 months, you may have had a headache, perhaps a little backache, or toothache. You may have experienced the pain of losing a friend who has died or the pain of loss, divorce or separation. If patients know a little more about their pain, what causes it, and what can be done about it, they will be able to help their doctor, nurses and pharmacists to give them the best possible care. In this book we intend to provide useful information to help you cope and hopefully, experience as little pain as possible. There is much that can be done!

2 WHAT IS PAIN AND WHAT CAUSES PAIN?

Many people think that to experience pain there must be some damage to the body. This is often true and this book discusses the many and varied causes of pain, which are often described as physical, psychological, social, emotional, spiritual and cultural.

It seems that all warm-blooded animals experience pain. It is useful for any animal to know when a part of its body is being injured so that it can avoid the cause. Indeed, it is necessary to be able to experience pain. In some medical conditions such as diabetes, the feet and legs can become numb. This means that a usually harmless condition such as an in-growing toenail or a thorn in the sole of the foot can become serious due to the development of an infection, because the toenail or the thorn was not noticed due to the lack of any pain. The damage can become widespread and serious before any action is taken.

The ability to sense sudden pain is therefore important but if the pain becomes repetitive or persistent due to progressive disease, then it is harmful to both physical and emotional well-being and serves no useful purpose. It can cause depression, anxiety and emotional and social breakdown. Persistent pain can cause its own increased sensitivities so that the sensation of pain becomes both more intense and more prolonged even after a single brief stimulus. Doctors call this *wind-up* and it is an important factor in persistent and long-lasting pain. The central nervous system – the brain and spinal cord – is adaptable and it can 'tune in' to an area that has been previously hurt and develop a kind of fast track to alert the brain to a sensation in this part of the body. Eventually, it can mean that even a light touch on the skin is interpreted by the brain as pain.

As well as pain caused by external factors and by disease, damage to the nervous system can also cause pain. Injury to the spinal cord can set up pain that is persistent. Many patients who have had a stroke develop pain. They may also be less able to sense temperature on the affected side. The onset of pain can be delayed for several years after the stroke. It can often be severe and be accompanied by the type of oversensitivity mentioned above, so that touch or even emotions can cause severe pain.

Assessment of pain is complex and often can be very difficult, even for a patient who is able to describe exactly what is being felt. The difficulties are much greater when dealing with infants and young children who can not tell you what they are feeling and with the elderly and the demented. With both these groups one has to assume that pain is being felt if it is known that similar disease in older, conscious adults would be likely to cause pain. Non-verbal signals such as facial expression and the way we sit can often be valuable in assessing both the degree of pain and the response to pain-killing measures. These non-verbal signals are best interpreted by the family or carers who have been closest to the patient. With the demented, it is possible to make the situation worse by giving pain-killing drugs and yet they should not be withheld solely for this reason. It requires the finest judgement to achieve pain relief without unwanted side effects in such situations and the help of a specialist team such as from a hospice should be sought if giving relief from evident distress is proving difficult.

3 THE IDEAL CONSULTATION

When you go to see your doctor or nurse about your pain, this should feel like a conversation between equals rather than an interrogation. The reason for going to see your doctor when you are in pain is to ensure that you get the best possible treatment. The doctor has a responsibility to give you enough time to explain all about your pain, to collect enough information to make an informed diagnosis, and to prescribe the most useful medication or other treatment.

It would be most helpful if you could tell the doctor everything he or she may need to know to help. Some things may seem trivial to you, but it is essential that you tell your doctor everything. If the doctor uses any words that you don't understand, you should ask to have these explained. Take as much time as you need. Time invested in your consultation is time well spent. You should never feel you are wasting the doctor's time.

Before you go to see the doctor, and afterwards, you may like to write down some questions. When we are nervous we tend to forget.

Your doctor or nurse will probably ask you some of the following questions:

- Tell me about your pain.
- Can you show me where it hurts, perhaps you can point to it?
- Does it hurt anywhere else?
- Can you describe the pain?
- What words would you use to describe the pain?
- When did it start?
- Is it there all the time or does it come and go?
- What makes the pain worse?
- What makes the pain better?
- How does the pain affect your day-to-day life?
- How does the pain affect your sleep and rest?
- Are you taking any medications for your pain?
- Do they help?
- Do you notice any problems when you take these medicines?

- Are you taking anything that has not been prescribed by the doctor, for example from a pharmacy or supermarket?
- Is there anything else you do that relieves the pain?

When you leave the surgery and think of a question you should have asked the doctor feel free to return or phone the surgery. Your pharmacist is an expert in the use of medications so don't hesitate to ask for advice.

Pain diaries

The doctor or nurse may ask you to 'measure the pain' by filling in what we call a rating scale or diary. It may look something like this:

0 _____ 10

No pain   Worst pain imaginable

You will be asked to mark the line at the position that represents how much pain you are feeling. Some patients find it helpful when their pain is being assessed, and also as a way of seeing if their pain is getting any better or worse with treatment. Others find that keeping such a diary causes them to think about their pain all the time. They may also feel anxious that they are letting the doctor down if they don't keep their diary up to date. However, this is just one way of measuring pain; your doctor or nurse may use other types of pain scales.

Sometimes doctors ask more then one question at a time, for example: 'What makes the pain worse or better, and is it worse at night?' Make sure that you answer all the questions you are asked.

The checklist in the next section may help you to ensure you get the best possible pain control from the team who look after you. If you think of any other questions, add them to the list.

4   PATIENT CHECKLIST

- Have I told the doctor everything about my pain?
- Has my doctor thoroughly examined me?
- Have I discussed any fears, worries or concerns about my care or treatment?
- Did I understand everything I have been told?
- Do I need to make another appointment?
- Has the doctor prescribed tablets or other medications?
- Has the doctor told me about all available medicines?
- Did he explain exactly how to use the medications he prescribed?
- Did I tell the doctor about other medications I take?
- Do I fully understand about the medications prescribed?
  - What they are called?
  - What are they for?
  - How should I store them?
  - What to do if I forget to take a dose?
  - When do I take them?
  - What side effects may I experience?
  - Is there any way I can avoid side effects?
  - What do I do if I get side effects?
- Have I talked to my doctor about other things I do to relieve my pain?

5 TYPES OF PAIN

Pains differ in many ways. It is very helpful for the doctor and nurse when a patient can describe his pain in as much detail as possible.

The *type* of pain is most important. It may be described as boring, nagging, stabbing, shooting, crushing or aching. You may use other words to describe your pain. It is very helpful to record the *intensity* or strength of pain. As in the pain diary or scale mentioned in Chapter 3, pain can be graded from 0 – no pain at all – to 10 – the worst possible imaginable pain. More complicated methods have also been described such as the McGill Pain Inventory and the Milan Integrated Pain Score. Generally, the simple tools are better.

The *timing* of the pain is equally important. Does it come on at rest, with movement of a limb, on weight-bearing, on deep breathing, or with activity? Is it after meals or during the passage of urine or motion? If the patient is already taking medication for the pain, is it effective, and if so for how long before the pain returns?

The *location* in the body where the pain is felt is obviously important. However, it can often happen that a problem in one part of the body is felt as pain elsewhere. For example, angina due to insufficient supply of oxygen into the heart is frequently felt as pain in the left arm. Compression of a nerve in the spine by a prolapsed intervertebral disc (slipped disc) gives the leg pain known as sciatica.

Such questions and their answers are the bedrock of getting precise diagnosis and effective relief. They depend upon the doctor or nurse asking them, and having time to evaluate each pain in turn, and also they depend upon the patient being able to answer accurately and objectively. Unfortunately many patients do not 'tell it how it is' but will exaggerate or minimise the pain either to emphasise its importance or to give an answer that will please the doctor. Both cultural and personal factors will influence how patients describe their pain.

Evaluating or monitoring the effects of pain treatments can be influenced by such things as the approach of the doctor, the patient's hopes, fears and view of the likely outcome of treatment, the wish to please the doctor, and the placebo effect. Simply taking any medication can

Home Record Diary

Date	Where is the pain?	How bad is the pain? (0–10)	Other symptoms			Description of the pain
			Constipation	Nausea/ vomiting	Daytime drowsiness	
25/10	Stomach	8	✓	✓		Intense, gnawing, miserable, unbearable
30/10						
4/11						

Current Medication Diary

Date	Drug name	Dose	How often?	Comments	Change of drug or dose; Date
25/10	Durogesic	25 mcg per hour	Every 3 days	Feel better. Less constipation, not as drowsy	
16/12				Pain controlled again. Feeling well, not needed laxatives	Increased dose to 50 mcg per hour patch on 1/12

help, particularly if we think it will help or we are told it will help. This does not mean that we are neurotic or susceptible to quackery. Many people will respond to a placebo, an inert substance, and percentages of responders vary – in five trials of 525 patients, between 7 and 38% of patients on a placebo obtained 10% of the maximum possible relief and 16% obtained more than 50%. Trials done to relieve pain from wisdom tooth extraction by the use of ultrasound showed that both pain relief and the reduction of swelling were equally effective *whether the ultrasound machine was switched on or off!*

Pain terms

Pain is divided anatomically into two types: *nociceptive and neuropathic.* All over the body there are sensory organs in the tips of nerves that detect pain. These are called nociceptors. They transmit nerve impulses via the spinal cord into the brain. The frequency and intensity of these impulses tell us where the pain is, how bad and what type it is. They will frequently produce a reflex muscular response to avoid the painful stimulus, e.g. a leg jumping away from a burning surface, or a hand quickly letting go of a red-hot pan handle, without any conscious decision being taken to move it.

In pains caused by disease, the nociceptors are stimulated directly by the disease process. Some tissues, e.g. the eye and the fingers and toes, are richly supplied with nociceptors so that even very slight trauma or the early stages of a disease will cause severe pain. Other organs, such as the liver, have very few nociceptors and will respond to extensive disease with little or no pain, unless the capsule is involved.

When such stimuli reach the spinal cord they can be magnified so that the brain is 'tuned in' to that sensation and responds more actively. They can also be damped down or even blocked completely by inhibitory messages coming down the spinal cord from the brain.

The second main type of pain is *neuropathic* pain. It is caused by nerves that carry messages of sensation, including pain, light, touch, vibration, warmth and coldness, being compressed or damaged by disease or an accident. The pain is then felt in the area of the body supplied by that nerve. An example of this is the pain caused by the *herpes zoster* (shingles) virus, which can lie dormant on a nerve for years or decades and then suddenly become active. The pain is felt in blisters arising in the nerve's territory and the pain can persist long after the skin has healed. Another neuropathic pain is that of Pancoast's syndrome. Here a cancer in the tip of one lung spreads upwards between or through the first and second ribs to involve the brachial plexus. This is a set of nerves that carry sensation from the whole arm. The result is a painful, numb, weak hand and forearm.

6   INVESTIGATING PAIN

This section explains the types of tests that may be carried out to diagnose the cause of pain, such as:

- blood tests
- x-rays
- CAT scans
- MRI scans
- myelograms.

Investigation in medical terms means the use of tests to confirm the diagnosis that has been made by talking to the patient and doing a careful physical examination. Tests are also used to rule out other conditions that may be related to the main illness and which may complicate its treatment. For example, a routine chest x-ray might reveal a hidden lung tumour which would seriously complicate recovery from an operation to replace a painful arthritic hip.

Blood tests

These fall into two main groups. Haematology looks at red cells, white cells and platelets which are circulating in the blood. Biochemistry, which screens the minerals in the blood, checks on liver and kidney function and looks for particular substances such as specific factors for rheumatoid arthritis, some cancers and acute inflammation or infection. Taking samples and testing over a period of time will usually show whether treatment of the disease has been effective. Many blood tests are simple, cheap and very effective. The results are usually made available very quickly.

Imaging

For many years, the only way of looking inside the body was by the use of x-rays. X-rays are still very useful, being able to show many structures, particularly bone and joints, in fine detail. They are quick, cheap, readily available and non-invasive. However, since they are a form of radiation, their use should be restricted to necessary investigations only.

CAT (computerised axial tomography)

Scans also use x-rays but computers allow us to build up a series of 'slices' through the body, usually about 1 cm apart. These show tissues such as muscle, kidneys, liver, heart and brain in more detail than ordinary x-rays, and can detect small abnormalities in parts of the body. This is very useful, as it is sometimes difficult to detect the early stages of diseases in areas deep inside the body. CAT scanning is also used to guide doctors who are carrying out certain procedures, such as obtaining a piece of tissue (a biopsy) from inside the body so that it can be looked at under a microscope or tested for bacterial infection. Although it has advantages, CAT scanning is more expensive than ordinary x-rays, it exposes the patient to more radiation and is not available in small hospitals. Waiting times can be long.

MRI (magnetic resonance imaging)

This technique uses magnetic rays rather than x-rays to obtain pictures. It is the most recent and powerful development of imaging techniques and produces pictures of great clarity, particularly of the brain and spinal cord, chest and abdomen. Sometimes it is necessary to inject a dye to show some tissues. MRI is often the first choice for rapid, accurate diagnosis and for monitoring progress. It can be repeated frequently because it does not use x-rays. However, it is very expensive and at present is only installed in the larger district general hospitals. This leads to long waiting times for MRI scanning, unless the need is obviously urgent or for something that is becoming more severe daily, such as a growing brain tumour. In such cases it is necessary for the professional in charge of the patient to arrange the MRI scan urgently by contacting the consultant radiologist.

Ultrasound

Ultrasound imaging uses high frequency sound waves which are reflected back from structures inside the body; the reflected sound waves are then used to build up a picture. It is very useful for distinguishing between fluid and solid objects such as the waters around a baby in the womb, or fluid in the chest or abdomen. Ultrasound is quick, cheap, readily available and harmless. It is excellent for monitoring the development of babies and for looking at organs, such as the liver, which are large and uniform in structure but which can contain an abscess or tumour.

7 TREATING PAIN – THE OPTIONS, THE PROS AND THE CONS

- Lifestyle treatments
- Medical treatments
- Surgical treatments
- Complementary treatments

Lifestyle treatments

Pain that continues for a long time can make living a normal life very difficult. It makes people feel much more tired and irritable. Consequently, relationships with friends, family and colleagues can come under strain. Our ability to work can be affected so it is important to think about what we can do ourselves and with others to make changes to the way in which we live.

What can I do for myself that may help to reduce my pain?

It can be very helpful to sit quietly and think about an average day, or week, and think about when you experience pain the most. If you feel able, it is worth keeping a very simple diary (see Table 7.1) so that you can look at it and see what you can do. Your doctor or nurse may also find this helpful.

You may not want to record so much detail and some days you may not wish to write anything. After a few days it is possible that some patterns will become clear. For example, if bathing is always painful, it may be quite simple to make some modifications to the bath or to get help with bathing. Another possibility is to take some medication about half an hour before the bath or painful event when you think the pain will become worse.

When you take a close look at your diary you may see other patterns. For example, your pain may increase as the day wears on. If this is the

Table 7.1 An example of a pain diary entry

Date	Time	Pain score 0–5	Activity	Comments
22/08/01	08.00	2	In bed	Comfortable
22/08/01	08.45	4	Bath	Much pain, can't get comfortable
22/08/01	09.30	3	Resting on bed	Took paracetamol
22/08/01	10.45	1	Talking with nurse	Felt good to talk
22/08/01	12.45	0	Sleeping	
22/08/01	15.00	2	Walking (cold wind)	Pain in face

case, careful planning to allow rest periods will help. It can be very hard for busy people to make time to rest. We often feel guilty about resting, especially during the day, and think that other people will judge us for this. This may be true, so talking with friends and family may help them to understand and support you. People find that if they are able to take a rest or nap during the day they are much more productive and will get much more done in a day.

Working life

If your working life is being affected by pain, it is worth considering what can be done about this. Most managers would rather try to help you than lose your valuable skills in the workplace. Talk to your manager if pain is a problem at work. It may be possible to adapt your working environment or work patterns to minimise your pain.

Case study

Mary is a 46-year-old former sales executive. Three years ago she had a bad car accident, which left her with severe back pain. She was unable to return to her former job and retrained to learn office skills. She worked in a cramped office and frequently had periods of sick leave when her back pain was bad. She was about to resign when she spoke with her manager. The manager immediately agreed to move her into a new office and together they sought advice from

> their local disability living centre. Mary was provided with new office furniture and remained as a highly valued member of staff.

Comment

Perhaps not all managers would be as accommodating and supportive but it is better to discuss your problems with a manager rather than take sick leave. Many problems may be solved or alleviated at little financial cost.

Physiotherapy

Physiotherapists, like other health care professionals, are concerned with enabling patients to get the most out of life. Their role in pain control is varied. They may be able to help you in the following ways:

- helping you to examine your lifestyle and understand better why you may be having pain;
- teaching you to deal with pain by adopting new postures, for example ways of sitting, lying, standing and walking;
- providing or advising on different walking aids or footwear;
- teaching you how to use walking aids properly and checking at intervals (we all tend to get into bad habits!);
- accessing, in the doctor's surgery or physiotherapy department, sophisticated equipment. Some of this is mechanical while much today is electrical. This equipment can help to reduce pain and swelling and encourage you to stretch and use muscles that have become weak or don't work effectively. Ultrasound and diathermy equipment can also help in this process.

If you see a physiotherapist you may spend a lot of time with them and develop a close supportive relationship. During this time you will have opportunities to discuss worries and feelings as well as ways of helping.

Occupational therapy

Some of the work of an occupational therapist is similar to that of a physiotherapist. The occupational therapist is also trained to help you to cope with pain and life in general. He/she will be aware of many things that can be done in your home or workplace that will make life easier. For example,

15

you may have pain when trying to complete everyday tasks in the kitchen. Devices are available to help you, for example, peel an orange, open a can, pour a kettle with ease and safely with less or no pain.

Larger changes may be made in the home. For example, many people experience pain when bathing or washing. Seats and lifts can make these everyday activities simple and comfortable. Ramps may be fitted for those who need a wheelchair.

Social work

Social workers can give people in pain a lot of support. They are experts in the complex world of financial benefits. Money, which may be available from different sources, can be used to make changes to the home to enable people to be more independent. For example, people with pain often find it more difficult to get about and may feel the cold more than people without pain. Grants can help with home heating. As well as arranging financial support, the social worker will provide psychological support to the patient in pain.

Working together

It can be seen that the work of the physiotherapist, occupational therapist and social worker are complementary. They work together very effectively as long as someone co-ordinates the work. Your GP or nurse will be able to advise you about how to get as much help as you need from these professionals.

Case study: working together

Mary is a 50-year-old lady who lives in a small semi-detached house in town. After a bad car accident she gets a lot of pain in her back and legs. The pain is not bad when she rests but is much worse when she tries to do anything about the house. Mary says the doctors and nurses at the hospital have been very good but she is having difficulty coping at home.

Sarah, her district nurse, spent a lot of time with Mary. Over a period of 3 months she arranged for Mary to see a social worker, occupational therapist and physiotherapist who did the following.

The social worker arranged for Mary to receive additional benefit to help with the day-to-day running of the house and to pay for taxi fares. The occupational therapist and physiotherapist arranged for home adaptations and a new wheelchair, which meant that Mary could get in and out of the house easily and comfortably. A stair lift and bath aids mean that Mary can bathe herself without help. Mary says these things have changed her life and given her back her dignity.

Voluntary services

Many different voluntary organisations exist to help people in pain. They are often organised to give help to a particular group of people with a particular disease, illness or problem, for example, the Motor Neurone Disease Association, the Multiple Sclerosis Society, the British Heart Foundation. Your local library can give you information about local volunteers who may be able to help with all manner of things such as shopping, transport, housework and friendship. Do be careful that you check that a volunteer is genuine; most are.

Counselling

Talking to friends and family members can help us feel better but people we know tend to give a lot of advice about what we should do. This advice is usually very well meant, but on occasions a little misguided. Talking over problems and feelings with a trained counsellor can be helpful for some people. Counsellors are trained to help individuals to think carefully about problems and to work out ways of solving problems themselves. Counsellors do not usually give advice, but they may give information to help us to choose the best way forward (see p. 33).

A typical session

During a typical counselling session, the counsellor will begin with some general discussion about yourself and how you feel. You will then be given an opportunity to talk about your pain. You should never feel under pressure to talk about anything if it feels uncomfortable to do so.

Skilled counsellors will give you opportunities to talk by using phrases such as:

- Tell me about the last time you had pain.
- How does the pain affect your relationship with your partner?
- What do you do when the pain is really bad?
- What do you think is the cause of this pain?

After spending time exploring your experience of pain, it is important to try to move forward and the following questions may be asked:

- If you could do one thing that would really make a difference to your pain what would that be?
- Do you think it would be helpful to meet again?

Costs and availability

Many general practices now employ counsellors on a full-time or part-time basis. They recognise the value of counselling and they also recognise that GPs do not have the time to sit with patients for long periods.

Not all practices employ counsellors and you may need to consider private counselling. Your local telephone directory or yellow pages will list counsellors. Personal recommendations are worth considering. Prices vary from £25 to £50 for a session and concessions may be available. Ask about costs before you commit yourself.

Medical treatments

It should never be forgotten that pain is a symptom, that is, something that the patient feels or experiences, and not a disease. It is essential that the cause of the pain is found and, if possible, treated. If a complete cure is impossible, then control or improvement of the disease should be attempted. Treating the pain with painkillers (analgesics) without attempting to find the cause is bad practice.

Lessons to be learned
- Pain requires a diagnosis.
- Pain which persists requires investigation and probably referral to a specialist to obtain a diagnosis.

- Rare diseases occur only rarely – but when they do the professional may be caught out.

Lessons to be learned
- A serious illness can mimic a trivial one.
- It is always when the doctor is very busy that the unexpected and potentially dangerous happens.
- The patient often tries to tell the doctor what is wrong.

Complete freedom from pain at all times is the gold standard. Mild pain should normally only require mild painkillers to control it, regardless of the cause, provided that the drug chosen is effective for that kind of pain.

More severe pains require more powerful drugs, which sometimes produce more side effects, while very severe pains require the most powerful drugs that we have available (such as morphine) and sometimes in large amounts. Using these types of drugs can cause anxieties in the patient and doctor. There is a real fear of morphine because patients imagine it is addictive, that they will require bigger doses, or that it must mean they are very near the end of their life. The doctor, too, may have similar worries, particularly if the illness is likely to be a long one. Cultural differences, previous experiences in themselves or in others, and legal regulations on the prescription of some drugs all combine to produce a set of conditions that make complete pain relief challenging.

Another problem is that frequently the pain only comes on with something like walking, weight-bearing or if a dressing change is attempted. To have such patients completely pain free during these incidents may mean that for the rest of the time they may be on too high a dose of pain-relieving drugs.

The analgesic or pain ladder

In 1986, the World Health Organization put forward its Analgesic Ladder, a simple, reliable and effective way of understanding pain management. This included the steps outlined below.

(The word 'opioid' is used to describe a pain-killing drug that is chemically and medically similar to morphine, which is extracted from the opium poppy. Some of these drugs are very powerful and others are milder, so these are then described either as Strong Opioids or as Weak Opioids. Other pain-killing drugs, such as paracetamol or aspirin, which have no similarity at all to morphine, are called Non-Opioids).

- *Step 1*   Patients with *mild pain* should be treated with a non-opioid painkiller combined with additional drugs if necessary.
- *Step 2*   Patients with *moderate pain* and those who are not pain free on step 1 should be treated with a weak opioid drug often combined with an additional non-opioid drug.
- *Step 3*   Patients with *severe pain* or who fail to be pain free on step 2 should receive a strong opioid, if necessary combined with a non-opioid drug.

This ladder method of treatment has been tested over the last 15 years. Although originally introduced for the treatment of cancer pain, it is

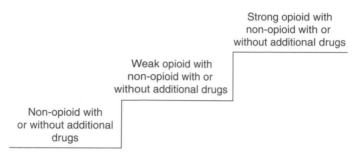

Figure 7.1 The analgesic or pain ladder

equally useful in dealing with non-cancer pains. The additional drugs mentioned are those that help pain relief, although they are usually prescribed for other reasons. Antidepressants, anticonvulsants, cortico-steroids and anaesthetic agents are all used in this way and can often be extremely valuable.

Non-opioids

The non-opioid painkillers that are used are normally either *paraceta-mol* or *aspirin*. Paracetamol is usually preferred as it is not as toxic as aspirin. It works in the central nervous system by blocking the feeling of pain but has no anti-inflammatory effect and therefore is unhelpful in diseases such as rheumatoid arthritis. Both aspirin and paracetamol will last only 4 hours and therefore frequent dosing is required to obtain continuous pain relief. The frequently prescribed 'four times a day' routine is therefore not enough for many patients.

Weak opioids

Weak opioids are drugs such as *dihydrocodeine*, which is similar to codeine but is more powerful although less well absorbed. It is usual to prescribe 30–60 mg every 4–6 hours but many patients feel very confused on 60 mg and sometimes 30 mg every 3 hours is tolerated better. There is also a slow-release preparation of this drug available in many countries. Like codeine, dihydrocodeine can be constipating, but unlike codeine, it must be given with caution to patients who have impaired kidney function.

21

Dextropropoxyphene is derived from methadone and is often prescribed in a compound tablet with paracetamol (co-proxamol or Distalgesic). This is effective for moderate pain and 1 or 2 tablets every 6 hours will give good pain relief in many patients. Elderly people find side effects such as sedation and sometimes constipation are distressing and overdosage combined with alcohol can be dangerous. *Tramadol* is a new painkiller, which can be given by mouth, rectally as suppositories, or by injection. Side effects such as headache, nausea, vomiting and dizziness are unusual but can occur. If nausea or vomiting become a problem, then this can be prevented by giving the antidote haloperidol at night.

Strong opioids

About 200 years ago, extracts from the opium poppy *Papaver somniferum* became available in the western world from China. It was quickly realised how valuable an analgesic this preparation was. Its potential for abuse leading to addiction caused morphine and similar drugs to fall under a cloud. In Great Britain, legislation was passed to control the prescribing and distribution of all the strong opioids and, sadly, at the same time the general public became frightened of morphine.

The medical use of morphine continued, however, but it was thought that it had to be combined in a 'cocktail' with other substances, particularly alcohol and cocaine. This was the original Brompton Mixture, famously criticised by Professor Patrick Wall, an internationally recognised expert on pain. He said:

> It is a disgraceful episode in the history of medicine that doctors and scientists allowed themselves to join a mass hysteria which confused the tremendous benefits of narcotics for the patient in pain with the social abuse of the same compounds.... The Brompton Mixture is a pitiful example of unthinking medicine ... a genuine cocktail of alcohol, cocaine and morphine ... no wonder the population was suspicious when a group of doctors declared that three social evils (booze, snow and dope) were good for you.

It was Dame Cicely Saunders, the founder of the modern hospice movement in the United Kingdom, who put the treatment of patients with morphine onto a rational and scientific footing and who demonstrated by her research that morphine given by mouth every 4 hours was effective and far more free of side effects than the traditional cocktails.

Morphine must be given regularly if pain is not to break through, and for patients with severe long-lasting pain, complete prevention is the only acceptable standard. Morphine should therefore be given by mouth and it should be given regularly. We know that it is effective for 4 hours; therefore, it must be given every 4 hours. Originally we had only morphine liquid but morphine tablets are now available and are much more acceptable as they are far less bitter than the liquid.

Four-hourly dosing is inconvenient and easily forgotten. Therefore the introduction of slow-release morphine was a great advance and we now have tablets that will last either 12 hours or 24 hours once the required dose has been established. More recently, long-lasting morphine granules have become available so that patients who have difficulty swallowing tablets can still have a long-acting preparation.

The side effects of morphine are divided into those that affect the normal working of the body (the *physiological* effects), and those that actually cause damage (the *toxic* effects).

Physiological effects

Most patients, when prescribed morphine or other opioid drugs, will feel more sleepy for the first 3–5 days. They will tend to nod off if nothing exciting or stimulating is happening. Their ability to think and perhaps talk with others may be a little impaired. This usually wears off after a few days, although it can persist in some patients.

Almost everybody taking morphine or related drugs will become constipated to some degree and therefore a laxative should be prescribed at the start of morphine treatment. It is not good enough to wait until constipation has set in before prescribing laxatives because

---

Case study

A man with advanced lung cancer was admitted to a hospice with severe abdominal pain which was not relieved by morphine even though the dose had been steadily increased. He had been given no laxatives and was severely constipated. Morphine was reduced and stopped and after energetic measures to relieve his constipation he was discharged home, pain free and on no painkillers.

by that time there are hard 'rocks' in the bowel, which require enormous contractions to expel them. If stimulant laxatives such as senna are given in these cases of constipation, they will cause severe colicky pain and if softening laxatives such as lactulose are prescribed, then frequently diarrhoea occurs as the laxative leaks uncontrollably around the 'rocks' in the bowel. Movicol is probably the best laxative to use for the prevention and treatment of this type of constipation.

Lesson to be learned

* Symptoms can often be due to side effects of treatment rather than to the original disease.

The third common side effect of morphine is nausea or feeling sick, often coupled with vomiting or being sick. Two-thirds of all patients who have not taken opioids before will experience this side effect. It can be prevented in almost all of them by giving a drug called haloperidol. Occasionally a patient will also need another drug, metoclopramide, to help empty the stomach. Characteristically, the nausea caused by morphine is not relieved by being sick. Even when the stomach is completely empty, the patient constantly feels sick and is convinced that at any minute he will be sick. Constant dry heaving and retching can be most distressing. Once encountered, many patients will never again agree to take morphine. Taking haloperidol, particularly in the old and frail, is advisable before introducing even a small dose of morphine.

Toxic effects

The toxic effects of morphine are completely different. They occur when a patient is being over-treated either because the dose is too big, because their kidney function is poor and they cannot get rid of it from the body, or occasionally because another painkiller has been given as well to a patient already on morphine. In this situation the patient is not mildly sleepy but can fall fast asleep and be almost unrousable, even when talking. When awake, the patient may have vivid visual hallucinations, which they often conceal because they think they are going out of their mind. They see people, animals, insects, particularly around the edges of the field of vision. Two physical signs are frequently observed in morphine toxicity. These are pinpoint pupils and jerking of the hands and forearms.

Other strong opioids

Fentanyl

This man-made opioid is more powerful than morphine, and is used to treat cancer pain. It is not well absorbed by mouth and therefore used to be given by injection, particularly for pain after operations. However, a novel patch formulation, worn on the skin like a sticking plaster, has been produced and is marketed as Durogesic. Patches are a relatively new way of giving medicines where the drug is gradually absorbed through the skin. This allows fentanyl to be given in very small doses across the skin. Such tiny doses are needed because fentanyl enters the brain very much more readily than does morphine. A minute dose is therefore sufficient. Because the patch takes 24 hours to become effective, this type of drug delivery, which is known as transdermal, meaning 'across the skin', is not suitable for a patient with untreated existing pain. It has therefore usually been necessary to start the patient on morphine, in order to establish the dose required, and then transfer to fentanyl. However, more recently, research has shown that it is possible to transfer directly from a weak opioid to a fentanyl patch and to obtain adequate pain relief quite rapidly. Fentanyl is claimed to be less constipating, less sedative and perhaps less nauseating than morphine; indeed, some patients on fentanyl complain of excess wakefulness, particularly if they have become used to the sedative effects of continuous morphine.

Hydromorphone

Hydromorphone is very popular in North America and is also available in the United Kingdom as Palladone. It is seven times more powerful than morphine and is often tolerated better. Both rapid-release and slow-release preparations are available.

Methadone

This is an old, very cheap drug, often used to wean addicts off heroin. In recent years there has been considerable interest in the medical profession for using methadone when treatment with morphine has failed or was inappropriate, for example in severe kidney failure. However, methadone is a difficult drug to use because it has a very long life in the body, it builds up when given regularly, and there is not a consistent relationship between the relief of pain and the amount of methadone in the circulating blood. It is therefore a drug to be used by specialists in pain relief and not by those with little or no experience of using it.

Case study

A 72-year-old man with advanced lung cancer required strong pain relief towards the end of his life. He was an academic whose aim was to remain in total mental control of his illness and his body for as long as possible. When taking a non-steroidal anti-inflammatory drug (NSAID) and morphine he was pain free, but found that his brain would not function as it normally did. He could not keep up intellectual discussions with his friends when they visited him and he greatly disliked this. When changed to fentanyl, his pain relief was equally effective but his brain regained full activity. He was able to do the Times Crossword in his usual 8.5 minutes.

Case study

A 68-year-old man had advanced prostate cancer. Pain from this was controlled with a non-steroidal anti-inflammatory drug together with radiotherapy but he then suffered a stroke. This left him mildly demented although fully active. He could hold a simple conversation, feed himself and remain continent. As the cancer progressed, he required stronger pain relief and when morphine was introduced he became aggressive, noisy, dirty and uncooperative even though it got rid of the pain. His wife, who cared for him devotedly, was greatly distressed by this change in his personality. His medication was changed from morphine to the equivalent dose of fentanyl and on this he remained pain free but regained his normal sunny disposition.

Lessons to be learned
- Relief from pain is not enough if accompanied by distressing or unacceptable side effects.
- A change from one painkiller to another may be equally effective in relieving symptoms while avoiding the unwanted side effects.

Clinical trials comparing fentanyl and morphine have been carried out. It was found that more patients preferred fentanyl than morphine. It should be recognised that transfer from morphine to fentanyl may occasionally cause morphine withdrawal syndrome, with the patient becoming distressed and anxious, sweating profusely, feeling very unwell, and sometimes having dramatic diarrhoea. These symptoms are easily and effectively treated by giving small doses of morphine, decreasing in amount and frequency over 3–5 days.

Pethidine

Pethidine is excellent when very short, intense pain relief is required as, for example, during childbirth. However, it has no part to play in the treatment of long-lasting pain for which it is both ineffective and toxic. It is metabolised by the body into a substance called norpethidine, and this can cause tremors, jerking, agitation and eventually convulsions.

Additional drugs used in pain relief

Non-steroidal anti-inflammatory drugs (NSAIDs)

These drugs are invaluable in relieving many pains from toothache to arthritis. They all work by blocking an enzyme which produces inflammation and consequent pain in tissues. The ones most commonly encountered are ibuprofen (Brufen, Nurofen), diclofenac (Voltarol) and naproxen (Naprosyn). They are all cheap, readily available and convenient. All have some risk of producing dyspepsia or upset stomach, vomiting, gastric ulceration and occasionally gastric bleeding. The side effects can range from mild inconvenience to life-threatening. A further, much rarer side effect is progressive kidney failure. In addition, fluid retention can sometimes lead to heart failure. NSAIDs can interact with other drugs, such as anticoagulants, tablets for diabetes and digoxin, a heart pill. The gastrointestinal side effects of the NSAIDs can be largely prevented by using the smallest dose that is effective, by avoiding other drugs that can make side effects worse and by giving as antidote a drug such as omeprazole, lansoprazole or rabeprazole.

Corticosteroids

This is a group of drugs that are produced from the naturally occurring steroid hormone, hydrocortisone. When it was first used, hydrocortisone caused a dramatic improvement in patients' pain, particularly if they had diseases such as rheumatoid arthritis. However, it was quickly realised that the benefits were largely outweighed by the side effects of long-term steroid treatment. This included weight gain, high blood pressure, diabetes, and degeneration of the hip joints. Since that time, the pharmaceutical industry has tried to discover other corticosteroids that would give the benefits without the side effects. Of those currently available, *prednisolone* is the one most generally favoured. It can be very effective in relieving a wide variety of pains, including those caused by trapped nerves, arthritis, and headache due to brain tumours.

There are many other indications for the use of corticosteroids. The benefits can be dramatic in the short term but long-term treatment does carry some or all of the risks mentioned above. These are made more likely if steroids are given with some other anti-inflammatory drugs.

An even stronger corticosteroid is *dexamethasone*, which has all the benefits and all the side effects of prednisolone to a greater degree.

Anti-epileptic drugs

Since pain sensations are carried by nerves, it is logical that drugs which interfere with nerve conduction can sometimes lessen pain. Anti-epileptic drugs work by reducing the frequency and intensity of these nerve impulses. For some pains, particularly those associated with nerve injury, such as pain after shingles, trapped nerves due to slipped discs or cancer in the spine, and the rare but acutely painful condition known as trigeminal neuralgia of the face, anti-epileptics can be very valuable. These include *carbamazepine*, which is often effective but frequently causes sedation, particularly in the elderly. Therefore the dose has to be increased only very slowly to achieve a tolerable level that is effective. *Sodium valproate* is less sedative and can often be better tolerated. The dose also can be increased more quickly. *Gabapentin* is a newer anti-epileptic drug, which has very little sedative effect and therefore the dose can be increased very rapidly until it relieves pain. This is probably now the drug of choice and, although more expensive than the older ones, most patients find it the best to use for these conditions.

Antidepressant drugs

These are thought to work in a different way by increasing messages that come down the spinal cord from the brain and help to block out pain. They work upon the spinal cord and their use does not mean the patient

28

is in any way depressed. Of the available antidepressants, the older ones such as *amitriptyline* are more effective than the newer ones such as *fluoxetine (Prozac)* and *paroxetine (Seroxat)*. Unlike the treatment of depression, these drugs work on nerve pain very rapidly and usually in much smaller doses than those needed to treat depression. The disadvantages of amitriptyline are sleepiness, particularly in the elderly, as well as blurred vision, difficulty in passing urine, and constipation. There is also a tendency for the same dose to build up over several days or weeks. There is considerable risk to the heart if amitriptyline is taken in overdosage.

Antispasmodics

Much pain encountered in everyday practice is due to spasm of different parts of the body. Everybody has experienced the intense pain of colic due to rhythmic contractions of the bowel. Even if it is due to diarrhoea, this pain can be severe. Simple and even strong painkillers such as morphine are often not effective in relieving colic. However, drugs that work particularly on the muscles of the gut, such as *loperamide (Imodium)* and *hyoscine butylbromide (Buscopan)*, are extremely effective in blocking this pain if, of course, the cause of it can not be found and relieved. Similarly, bladder pain can be distressing. If possible, the cause, such as retention of urine or blockage due to a large prostate gland, should be relieved by passing a tube into the bladder. If this is not possible, for example, if the pain is due to a large bladder tumour, then the muscles of the bladder must be relaxed and here a drug called *oxybutynin* can help. Muscles can go into spasm, either with cramp often felt at night, for which quinine is highly effective, or with painful spasms, particularly after a stroke. Here, *baclofen (Lioresal)* often works very well. As some patients find it makes them sleepy, it must be started in a very small dose at night and then slowly increased until benefits are achieved without intolerable side effects. The tranquillisers such as *diazepam (Valium)* can be very effective in relieving muscle pains or spasms. There has been some bad publicity about these drugs over the years, but used carefully they have a lot to offer.

Drugs which prevent breakdown of bone

These are known as *bisphosphonates*. Bone is a living tissue that is continuously breaking down and growing. In some conditions, such as osteoporosis, the breakdown stage is too active and the bones become weak and likely to fracture. These drugs work by slowing down the

29

breakdown stage by cells called osteoclasts, resulting in stronger bones. This beneficial effect is extremely useful in relieving pain due to Paget's disease, cancer in the bones, and some other conditions. These drugs can be taken by mouth but are most effective if given by injection. They last a long time so that they only need to be given once every 3–6 weeks. As well as relieving pain and preventing bones from breaking, these drugs may also prevent cancer cells from settling in bones. Therefore, as well as relieving pain, they may have an important role in preventing pain due to harmful events in the skeleton.

Radiotherapy

The best treatment for the relief of pain in cancer that has spread to bone is radiotherapy. It acts particularly on the cancer cells, killing them and reducing their ability to destroy bone. It is usually extremely effective and nowadays is very well tolerated. It does make patients feel tired and of course it is necessary to travel to a radiotherapy centre, almost always in a large city. Sometimes only a single dose is necessary but often patients are asked to attend for five to nine treatments. In sensitive parts of the body it may be necessary to give extremely small amounts many more times than that. Usually the treatment is focused on to the site of the pain, but if bone cancer is very widespread throughout the body it is possible to give a single dose to either the upper or lower half of the trunk and limbs at a single session. This can cause a sudden flare-up of pain, requiring more pain-killing drugs for a few days after the treatment has been given. After a few weeks it is possible to give a similar treatment to the other half of the body.

A newer way of giving radiotherapy is by the use of a radioactive isotope by mouth or injection. This is more expensive but it has the advantage that it can be taken to the patient's bedside rather than the patient having to travel to the radiotherapy centre. Only a single dose is required, but it can be repeated if the pain recurs. The usual isotope used is strontium-89. Similarly, the disadvantages are the possible sudden flare-up of pain after treatment and the high cost.

Surgical treatments

Various operations can be performed to relieve pain depending on its site and cause. Local injections of an anaesthetic such as *lignocaine* (as is employed all over the world by dentists to anaesthetise a dental nerve before starting work on a tooth filling), can be effective. However, lignocaine is quite short acting, so it is more usual for long-term relief to use a similar drug called bupivacaine. This is often combined with a corticosteroid such as prednisolone (see above). These injections can be put into soft tissue or muscles, to block nerves, or into painful joints. They are frequently effective although they do not cure pain. Another route sometimes used is to give *epidural* (around the spine) injections. This involves injecting a mixture of local anaesthetic and usually a corticosteroid drug around the outside of the membrane that encloses the spinal cord. The nerves which pass through this membrane are anaesthetised and the area which they serve is numbed either for a few hours or, if the epidural injection is continued by a continuous drip feed, the pain relief can be continued almost indefinitely. Another route is to give the same mixture of drugs inside that membrane so that the spinal cord itself is directly bathed in local anaesthetic. This technique is known as an *intrathecal injection.* It requires more experience to put it in and to service it afterwards, but the dose of drugs required is very much less than with the epidural route. If the pain is severe, then an opioid such as morphine or diamorphine can be added to the mixture. These techniques are used for relieving pain in the legs, the pelvis, or during childbirth.

Orthopaedic surgery can be very effective in relieving pain. The technique of complete replacement of arthritic hips, knees, shoulders and even wrists is now well established and produces superb relief for patients who have previously suffered severe pain. In cancer treatment, if a bone breaks because of cancer deposits, then surgeons can stabilise the fracture with a pin or nail inserted along its length. Even better is to realise that a fracture such as this is inevitable and therefore to nail or pin it *before* the fracture occurs. This requires vigilance and realisation of what is likely to happen. It is good practice, however, to act before the problem occurs.

Transcutaneous electrical nerve stimulation (TENS)

This clever medical device has been used for many years to help in the management of different types of pain. It has proved useful in pain due to trapped nerves as in sciatica and for people who get phantom limb pain after an amputation. Many hospices use TENS to help patients with some types of cancer pain.

The TENS equipment consists of three parts, the stimulator, the leads and the electrodes. The stimulator is powered by a 9 volt battery. The electrodes are made of carbon rubber. They are placed usually near the pain and the stimulator is adjusted to create a feeling of gentle but strong stimulation in the skin. Sometimes pain relief is immediate whilst in some people it may take time to be effective. The good thing about TENS is that you are in control. TENS will not be effective in all types of pain but it is worth talking to your doctor about it. He may refer you to a pain clinic if he thinks TENS will help.

It is possible to buy a TENS machine in some large chemists. We do not recommend this without medical advice.

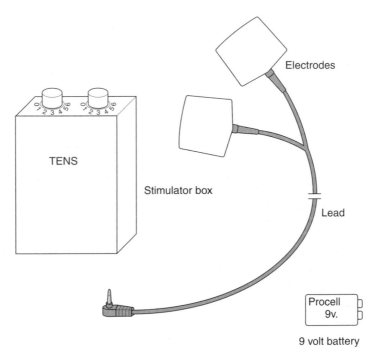

Figure 7.2   A transcutaneous electrical nerve stimulator

Complementary or alternative treatments

There are many complementary treatments (also known as alternative treatments) available today. We use the term complementary treatments, or therapies, because we believe their use should be considered alongside existing medical treatment rather than as alternatives.

It can be difficult to find strong evidence about how good these therapies are at relieving pain. This certainly does not mean that they do not have a place. Although evidence may not be available, it makes good sense to think about some of the more common complementary therapies and how they may be used to relieve pain.

We advise you to be very wary of any complementary therapy practitioner who tells you that they can cure you of your condition or tells you to stop taking medications or treatments prescribed by your doctor. If you decide to see a complementary therapist you should always do the following first: talk to your doctor or nurse; ask the therapist to

- explain the treatment and how it will help you;
- tell you exactly how much the treatment will cost;
- tell you how many sessions you are likely to need.

This book is not intended to explain fully all forms of complementary therapies but to give you a little information about some of the more common therapies and how they may help you.

Counselling, sometimes known as psychotherapy

Some people find it very helpful to talk to a friend or colleague about a problem, including pain. Unfortunately, friends are often too keen to tell us what to do. Whilst this can be helpful, counselling is different. Counselling aims to allow the patient or client to work out for themselves what is wrong and then to decide what to do about it. The first session with a counsellor may last an hour and a half with additional hour-long sessions. The first session will begin with introductions and you will be invited to talk about your pain in some detail. Don't be surprised if your counsellor says very little. A skilful counsellor knows how to help you to talk and to carefully listen to what you have to say.

At the following sessions, your counsellor will help you to think about various things you may be able to do that will help your pain. The counsellor is unlikely to offer advice and some people find this very strange, particularly when they have been cared for by the NHS, which is very busy and used to giving instructions and advice. Some people who experience counselling are quite surprised to find explanations for and ways of treating their pain they had never even thought of.

It is very important to realise that for some, counselling is not helpful. Some people find it very difficult to talk about a problem. If you are not finding it helpful you should tell your counsellor, who may then try a different approach or suggest a different counsellor or refer you back to your doctor.

Relaxation

Pain causes us to become tense and tension causes us to experience pain. Learning effective ways of relaxing can help to break this cycle.

Benefits of relaxation

- Lower pulse
- Lower blood pressure
- Lower temperature
- Less muscular tension
- Pain reduction
- Better rest and sleep
- Feeling better
- Feeling of being in control

Some people worry about side effects, but it does not appear that relaxation has any. Some people cope with their illness by being on their guard all the time. If someone like this is very relaxed, they could become upset and cry. This could be upsetting, but may offer a chance to talk about problems. Other people, when deeply relaxed, may experience feelings like floating, falling or spinning. Some find this unpleasant whilst others do not. If you feel like this, all you need to do is open your eyes and the feeling will soon pass.

Relaxation methods

People relax in may different ways, for example, watching television, walking, vigorous exercise, drinking alcohol, smoking, television, radio, music or a hot bath. Some of these may be thought of as less positive than others and some are difficult for very ill patients. The above methods are unlikely to create a state of deep relaxation but they may still be used if you get relief while using them.

Relaxation is a skill like learning to ride a bicycle and all skills need practice. Relaxation techniques are unlikely to be helpful in all circumstances. For example, if you are about to sit your driving test and you have not learned how to drive, relaxation will not help very much.

Ideal conditions for relaxation

The best conditions for relaxation require a bed or couch, warmth, privacy, individual attention and freedom from disturbance. It is often not possible to create such conditions but this should not discourage you trying to relax. Many people with a little practice will be able to relax deeply, even in 'busy' surroundings.

Some techniques to try are as follows.

Progressive muscular relaxation

You will be guided through a sequence of simple tensing and relaxing exercises so that you can become aware of the difference between tension and relaxation. It usually begins with tensing and relaxing hands and arms and then working from head to toe. If you have a painful area, do not tense this area as this will only make the pain worse.

Advantages and disadvantages are:

- This method is easy to learn. Many people have used it before, for example during childbirth or antenatal classes.
- Tension may increase pain or cause you to focus on one particular area.

Guided imagery or fantasy

You will be encouraged to think of relaxing images or pictures in your mind, such as a holiday scene or pleasant garden.

Advantages and disadvantages are:

- Some people can't visualise or imagine a relaxing scene.
- Time must be allowed for the image to develop.
- Some people may feel a little uneasy if they are not in control.
- Those who find visualisation difficult may feel 'put off' by the experience.
- Imagination has no boundaries so you can 'do' anything you want in your mind.

Hypnosis/hypnotherapy

The general public and many health care professionals often think of hypnosis as something mystical and magic. This is largely because of stage and television shows. Hypnotherapy takes the patient into a deep state of relaxation. In that state you will be open to positive and beneficial suggestions. Hypnotherapy has been found to be useful for some types of pain and other distressing feelings such as sickness and anxiety.

Hypnotherapy is a safe and effective approach but should only be used by those who have been specifically trained. As always it is important to discuss hypnotherapy with your doctor.

Meditation

Meditation is another approach to relaxation which requires the patient to practise quiet relaxation. A mantra is sometimes used to deepen the relaxation. A mantra is usually a 'neutral' sound without any meaning. It is repeated silently over and over again. This helps the user to concentrate their thoughts and almost block out the outside world. Concentrating on objects such as a candle in a darkened room or a flower or a pleasant smell are useful alternatives to the mantra.

Deep breathing

Teachers of relaxation often ask their subjects to 'focus on their breathing', 'become aware of their breathing' or 'notice their breathing'. This is undoubtedly helpful for many patients but could be unhelpful if you have a breathing problem.

Dealing with distractions

When someone attempts to relax, they may be bothered by distractions such as worries or thoughts going through their mind. This may make relaxation difficult and can put people off. Some suggest that we should 'clear the mind' or 'not concentrate on anything'. This may be helpful for some people but in practice it can be difficult to do. Try not thinking of the colour red! Alternatively, try simply staying with the thought/concern, rather than trying to push it out of your mind.

Some people are put off using relaxation techniques because they say they do not have enough time. The 5-minute technique set out below in Figure 7.3 is easy to learn and easy to use. You may like to get

Find a comfortable position, sitting with your feet flat on the floor or lying down, hands by your sides. 'I will count down from 10 to 0 and, by the time I reach 0 you will feel very relaxed.'

TEN	*feeling your body becoming heavy*	*sinking into the floor*
NINE	*legs relaxed.*	
EIGHT	*trunk relaxing*	
SEVEN	*chest relaxed*	
SIX	*arms feeling heavy.*	*hands warm.*
FIVE	*shoulders and neck relaxed*	
FOUR	*head relaxed*	
THREE	*jaw relaxed*	
TWO	*more and more relaxed*	*deeper and deeper*
ONE	*the whole body is relaxed*	*deeper and deeper*
	more and more relaxed	
ZERO	*more and more relaxed*	*warm and peaceful*

'Now I will count back up to 10 again. When I reach 10, open your eyes, move your fingers and toes and very gently stretch. 0, 1 ,2, 3 ,4, 5, 6, 7, 8, 9, 10.

Now keep the relaxed feeling with you as you move around and carry out your activities.'

Figure 7.3 The 5-minute countdown technique

someone to read this slowly to you or you can make a tape for yourself. Feel free to change the script to suit yourself.

Aromatherapy

Aromatherapy involves the use of pleasant smelling oils, sometimes known as essential oils. They can be administered in a number of ways including applying directly to the skin or clothes (after dilution), inhaling the oil, which has been vaporised in steam or in a cold compress. It is possible to buy aromatherapy oils from many shops although the quality may vary.

Some papers are now being published in professional journals that suggest aromatherapy oils can help by making patients feel more comfortable and relaxed. However, a lot of research still needs to be done.

It is worth talking to your doctor or nurse who may be able to advise you. Some patients may have unpleasant skin rashes if oils are applied directly to the skin. Oils should always be used with caution during pregnancy. Aromatherapy is not usually available as part of NHS care but it is sometimes available in hospices and day-care units. It is generally cheap and readily available, but check prices before you see an aromatherapist.

Massage

Massage has been used effectively for many years. Parents instinctively massage their children when they are in pain or upset. Gentle massage can help to reduce pain by creating a feeling of warmth and relaxation. Deeper massage, often applied, for example, by skilled physiotherapists, can help to reduce pain by loosening tense muscles, tendons and ligaments. In some cases it is possible to massage your own painful area and this has obvious advantages. Your friends and relatives may be able to massage you and they may like to help you by being involved in this way. Short massage courses are often provided in local schools and colleges and they are well worth attending to provide you with further skills.

Massage may be applied directly to the dry skin or alternatively, aromatherapy oils, creams or talc may be used to make the experience more enjoyable.

Acupuncture

This is an ancient form of treatment which involves inserting very fine needles below the skin on various parts of the body. Patients say they feel the needles going into the skin but, because they are so fine, most people do not find the experience unpleasant or painful. When the needles have been inserted, patients are usually left to rest for a while. Sometimes the needles are gently stimulated by turning, applying gentle heat or very small electric currents.

Acupuncture is thought to work in two ways. Western ideas suggest acupuncture works by helping the body to produce small amounts of morphine-like chemicals, called endorphins, which reduce pain. Eastern theory suggests that acupuncture balances energy within the body.

Many doctors and physiotherapists have done further training in the use of acupuncture and may be able to help you. Always ask your doctor and never go to an acupuncturist you don't know. It is essential that needles are correctly used and sterile so that infections are not passed between patients.

Homeopathy

This is an ancient form of medicine that uses minute doses of 'remedies' to treat a condition. A typical course of treatment involves an initial long consultation, during which you will be asked all about yourself and your pain. The homeopath is likely to prescribe one or more remedies to be taken for the next few weeks. Follow-up appointments will be needed to monitor progress and change treatments, if necessary. You may also be given advice about what to eat and how to get better rest and sleep.

Herbal medicine

Herbal medicine relies on the use of treatments derived from medicinal herbs to manage pain and other conditions. As with all complementary therapies, an initial consultation and follow-up appointments will be arranged for you. It is very important that you tell both your doctor and your herbalist about any drugs you are taking, even if they have not been prescribed by your doctor. We are often led to believe that herbal medicines are natural and safe, but it is possible that preparations may interact with each other. Also, not all 'natural' compounds are safe – belladonna berries are also called deadly nightshade.

Organisations providing useful information about complementary therapies

Council for Complementary and Alternative Medicine (CCAM)
63 Jeddo Road, London W12 6HQ
Tel: 020 8735 0632

British Complementary Medicine Association (BCMA)
249 Fusse Road South, Leicester LE3 1AE
Tel: 0116 282 5511

British Holistic Medical Association (BHMA)
59 Lansdowne Place, Hove, East Sussex BN3 1FL
Tel: 01273 725951

Institute for Complementary Medicine (ICM)
PO Box 194, London SE16 1QZ
Tel: 020 7237 5165

British Acupuncture Council
63 Jeddo Road, London W12 9HQ
Tel: 020 8735 0400

British Association for Counselling (BAC)
1 Regent Place, Rugby, Warwickshire CV21 2PJ
Tel: 01788 578328

Transcendental Meditation
FREEPOST, London SW1P 4YY
Tel: 0990 143733

British Herbal Medicine Association (BHMA)
Sun House, Church Street, Stroud, Gloucestershire GL5 1JL
Tel: 01453 751389

British Homeopathic Association (BHA)
27a Devonshire Street, London W1N 1RJ
Tel: 020 7935 2163

British Medical Acupuncture Society (BMAS)
Newton House, Newton Lane, Lower Whitley, Warrington, Cheshire
WA4 4JA
Tel: 01925 730727

International Society of Professional Aromatherapists
82 Ashby Road, Hinckley, Leicestershire LE10 1SE
Tel: 01455 637987

National College of Hypnosis and Psychotherapy
12 Cross Street, Nelson, Lancashire BB9 7EN
Tel: 01282 699378

8 COMMONLY ASKED QUESTIONS ABOUT PAIN

Pain is just something we all have to bear isn't it? Maybe it's payback time for wrongs I have committed.

Nobody should have to suffer unnecessary pain today. Some people, more often men than women, feel that it is a weakness if they cannot bear pain. This is a very unhelpful belief and likely to result in you experiencing unnecessary pain. If you feel that your pain is because you have done something wrong in your past perhaps you should talk this over with someone. This may be a good friend or a minister of religion. This is one time when it certainly is good to talk.

It says take two on the packet but I always try to take only one because I don't like taking tablets. This is much better for you isn't it?

Drug doses are very carefully worked out by the drug companies and qualified pharmacists. Doctors have experience in prescribing the right amount. If you take only half the dose the drug may not help your pain. Consequently you may think the drug is no good. You should always take the dose that has been prescribed, but if you do experience any side effects, then you should talk to your doctor, nurse or pharmacist immediately, since it is always possible that you may experience side effects that are uncommon.

I have heard that morphine is addictive. Is this true?

Sometimes people abuse strong painkillers like morphine. This means that they take the drug for its effect on their mind. When people take morphine to control pain they do not become addicted. Morphine is a very safe drug and can be given to control many types of pain.

I have heard that paracetamol is a very dangerous drug. My doctor has prescribed it to be taken regularly. I am very worried, so what should I do?

First you should tell your doctor you are worried and exactly why you worry. When taken as prescribed, paracetamol is a very safe drug. You may have heard that it is dangerous if taken in overdose and this is true. It is dangerous because it can cause damage to the liver. Normally your doctor will prescribe two tablets to be taken four times a day. You should not normally take more than eight tablets in 24 hours.

Will I be like a zombie if I take morphine?

For the first few days of taking morphine you may feel more drowsy than you did before. This may simply be because the drug is relieving your pain and therefore you feel more able to rest and sleep. If you continue to feel drowsy you should tell your doctor or nurse who may advise you to change the amount you are taking. It is also possible that other drugs or the strain of being ill may make you feel drowsy.

The doctor put my Dad on morphine when he was dying. Does this mean I am dying?

Of course some people who take morphine may be going to die in the near future. Equally, many patients who take morphine may have diseases that don't threaten their lives, such as arthritic pain. Taking morphine does not mean you are dying. Morphine is given to relieve pain. If you are worried about your future talk it over with your doctor or nurse. Tell them exactly what you worry about and what you want to know.

9   CASE STUDIES

John: a labourer with back pain

John is a 49-year-old labourer for a construction company. He visited his doctor complaining of back pain, which he had had for 4 weeks, and asked for painkillers and a sick note. However, his doctor suggested he saw the practice physiotherapist. Outraged, John asked to see another GP who advised the same approach.

John returned a week later to see a third GP who invited him to make a longer appointment the next day. John reluctantly agreed. The next day the GP asked John what he thought was causing the pain. John replied: 'that's bloody obvious when you have been humping around heavy loads over the years.' They talked generally for a few minutes after which the GP commented that John seemed very angry about something. The doctor invited him to make an appointment with the counsellor but John was not impressed. However, over the next few days, John thought about this and made his first appointment. At the weekly counselling sessions, John talked about how he felt as he approached 50 and the possibility of being pushed aside by young fit lads. John began an exercise regimen and took a long hard look at his life and his health. He started eating well and 'just enjoyed being 50'. Within a few weeks he had a completely different outlook on life and his back pain was much better.

Comment

It is very easy to look at pain as a physical thing. One GP considered the many factors which contribute to the experience of pain and sought other methods of managing John's pain.

Stephanie: a nurse with abdominal pain

Stephanie was 31 when she began to experience vague abdominal pain 1 week in every 4. She put this down to premenstrual syndrome. A visit to her GP met with a sharp response: 'You nurses are all the same, always something wrong with you.' Stephanie discussed her problem with her colleagues, and each had suggestions for remedies. She took vitamin B6, evening primrose oil, herbal water tablets, and raspberry leaf tea. Each seemed to help for a month or two and then the pain returned. She also noticed changes in her periods and a swollen tummy. Reluctantly, she went to see another GP in the practice who examined her thoroughly and referred her to a gynaecologist. Ovarian cancer was diagnosed and Stephanie is now being treated with surgery and chemotherapy.

Comment

Stephanie's case again illustrates the need to consider the person as a whole. The first GP saw Stephanie as someone with pain that had a psychological cause only.

Tom: a retired miner with lung cancer

Tom is 58. He is very proud of the fact that he was one of the north east's last miners. Lung cancer was diagnosed a month ago. Tom was told and appeared to accept the diagnosis but his wife, Annie, was and remains very upset. If anyone tries to talk to her about Tom's illness, she fights back her tears and attempts to change the subject. Annie has a part time cleaning job which takes her out of the house most mornings. When the GP or district nurse visits, Tom never complains of pain and he looks remarkably comfortable. If the doctor or nurse visits Tom when Annie is at home, she sits beside him and tries to answer any questions on Tom's behalf. Tom looks distressed and he has difficulty breathing. Annie insists he has something for the pain. The GP and district nurse arrange to visit together two days later. The GP examines Tom while the district nurse takes Annie into the kitchen to make a cup of tea. She says to Annie: 'This must be very difficult for you. Do you and Tom talk about the future?' Annie replies: 'Of course we do. We have always shared everything.' The district nurse says: 'Everything?'. Annie breaks down in tears and asks the district nurse what to do. The GP has been having a similar conversation with Tom. A few minutes later the four of them sit down to a cup of tea and a frank discussion about the future. The doctor and district nurse continue to visit regularly and Tom dies peacefully 6 weeks later. He never needs anything more than paracetamol for his pain.

Comment

Tom and Annie are a typical loving couple facing the pain of death and separation. Each is trying to protect the other from pain but both end up being hurt. Skilful care enables Tom and Annie to voice their concerns and to face the future together no matter how painful it is.

10 HELP AND INFORMATION – WEBSITES, CHARITIES AND SELF-HELP ORGANISATIONS

The Internet is being used increasingly by patients and their families who wish to learn more about their condition or problem. While it should never been seen as a substitute for good health care, the Internet is a rich source of useful information.

A few websites and newsgroups which you may find useful are listed below, but patients should always talk to their doctor or nurse about anything they find on a website. Sadly, sometimes people make claims about treatments that may be untrue. You should always be wary about ordering goods or materials on the Internet without first discussing them with your doctor, nurse or pharmacist.

Newsgroups allow anyone with access to a computer and the Internet to write a message or pose a question to all the other people who use the newsgroup. Newsgroups can be very useful if you want to ask a question or look for information. Please again be cautious. Often the people who reply are kind, sympathetic and understanding. At other times they can be rude and unhelpful. People may recommend medications or other courses of action which they have personally found useful. It is possible that their recommendations may have no scientific basis at all. The course of action they recommend may be harmful to you. One way to find these newsgroups is to visit a website called Deja. The website address is www.deja.com.

Websites

- For long-lasting pain: The American Chronic Pain Association at www.theacpa.org
- For cancer pain: Cancer Care at www.cancercare.org
- The American Pain Foundation at www.painfoundation.org
- Back Care: The National Association for Healthy Backs, formerly the

Back Pain Association, is a UK Charity which helps people manage and prevent back pain by providing advice, promoting self help, encouraging debate and funding scientific research into better back care. www.backpain.org

www.trinityqc.com/cancer/painrelief

Getting relief from cancer pain

This talks about many worries faced by the patient in cancer pain. The website offers very helpful information and useful tips to help you manage your pain.

www.cancerbacup.org.uk

CancerBACUP is an excellent British website, providing all manner of information about cancer for patients and professionals alike. There is a lot of information about cancer pain. Visitors to the site can ask questions which will be answered by the team.

Two examples of recent questions are:

- What is the highest dose of morphine you can have?
- What is a TENS machine? Can it help with cancer pain?

The visitor can read, on-line, BACUP's excellent patient information booklets. The one called 'Feeling better, controlling pain and other symptoms of cancer' may be useful. If you don't like to use a computer you can contact BACUP on Tel: 020 7696 9003; Fax: 020 7696 9002; Freephone: 0808 800 1234. Alternatively, you can write to BACUP at CancerBACUP, 3 Bath Place, Rivington Street, London EC2A 3JR.

11   CANCERBACUP'S PAIN MANAGEMENT SURVEY

This was carried out (September–October 2000) by giving question-naires to patients who contacted their helpline and by a nurse who visited patients at a leading London teaching hospital. The findings show that almost two-thirds of the cancer patients surveyed believe pain is inevitable. A summary of the findings suggests:

- 69% had pain because of their cancer and 77% because of their treatment;
- 54% were not told to expect pain and 43% did not ask for medication to control the pain;
- 54% were not involved in decision making about their pain medication and 53% said the advantages and disadvantages of pain treatment were not discussed;
- 67% had concerns about taking strong painkillers;
- 64% reported side effects due to medication, including nausea, vomiting, constipation and drowsiness;
- 44% said their overall pain management could have been improved.
- 10% of patients were aware that drugs could sometimes be given in the form of skin patches;
- given the choice, 60% of patients would prefer a skin patch to the other ways of taking medicines (e.g. injections, suppositories, tablets, liquid medicines).

This shows that there is a lot of room for improvement in the management of cancer pain although it should be remembered that some of the patients who consulted CancerBACUP may have had worse pain problems than other cancer patients.

CancerBACUP produced a freedom from pain charter. This was designed for cancer patients but is equally important for other patients in pain.

The charter

- People with cancer should not experience severe pain.
- Most pain caused by cancer or by treatment for cancer can be effectively controlled.
- Patients have the right to expect that any pain they experience will be effectively managed.
- Patients have the right to receive full information about the choice of all pain relief options available to them.
- Patients and health professionals should discuss fully the benefits and side effects of all different types of pain relief.
- Every patient should have access to high quality, accurate, unbiased information as recommended in the NHS Cancer Plan.
- Patients should participate fully in making decisions about their treatment leading to greater satisfaction.

12 SUMMARY

Throughout this book we have tried to explain pain and to suggest simple but effective ways of dealing with pain. We sincerely hope the book will help you. Here is a summary to help you remember the main points of the book:

- Pain is not inevitable and it can be treated.
- Talk about your pain, tell your doctors and nurses how you feel. Be sure the people who look after you really understand how you are.
- Understand your treatment. Ask again and again if you don't understand.
- Take your medicines as prescribed. If you get side effects don't give up, many will pass. Go back to your doctor and tell him/her.
- Think about what you can do to get control of your pain. Eat well, rest and sleep often and organise your life so that pain is not the most important focus in your life. The diary may help.
- Talk to your family and to your manager at work.
- Think about things other than medications that may help.
- Learn a relaxation technique. It will help.

INDEX